Carli Lloyd

By Jon M. Fishman

AMAZING ATHLETES

Lerner Publications ◆ Minneapolis

Lerner Publications Company
A division of Lerner Publishing Group, Inc.
241 First Avenue North
Minneapolis, MN 55401 USA

For reading levels and more information, look up this title at www.lernerbooks.com.

Library of Congress Cataloging-in-Publication Data

The Cataloging-in-Publication Data for *Carli Lloyd* is on file at the Library of Congress.
ISBN 978-1-5124-0866-9 (lib. bdg.)
ISBN 978-1-5124-0867-6 (pbk.)
ISBN 978-1-5124-0868-3 (EB pdf)

Manufactured in the United States of America
1 – BP – 12/31/15

TABLE OF CONTENTS

Carli Lloyd (*left, in white*) scores a goal against Japan in the final game of the 2015 World Cup.

WORLD'S BEST

Carli Lloyd sprinted to the goal. The ball bounced in from her right. She stretched with her left foot and punched the ball with her toes. It streaked into the net for the first goal of the game!

Carli and the United States Women's National Team (USWNT) were playing in the 2015 World Cup final game. It was a tough showdown against Japan. The winner would be the world champion. The game had just started, but Carli's goal helped her team relax.

Carli celebrates a goal against Japan.

A few minutes later, the USWNT was on the attack again. A US player passed the ball to the front of the net. Carli circled to her left as the ball bounced around. US and Japanese players kicked at it. But it came through to Carli. She jumped and tapped the ball into

Carli (*left*) fights to keep the ball from a Japanese player.

the net with the side of her foot. The US lead grew to two goals.

Fourteen minutes into the game, US player Lauren Holiday scored.

Japan couldn't slow down the USWNT. About two minutes after Holiday's goal, the ball bounced to Carli in the middle of the field. There were Japanese players all around her. With nowhere to go, Carli launched the ball toward the Japanese goal. It soared high above the field. The Japanese **goalkeeper** got her fingertips on the ball. But she couldn't keep it out of the net. Carli had scored a **hat trick** in just 16 minutes! She was the first woman to score a hat trick in a World Cup championship match.

Japan fought back. They knocked in two goals to make the score 4–2. But they couldn't score again. The United States won the game, 5–2. It was the first World Cup title for the USWNT since 1999.

Carli and her teammates danced on the field. They hugged one another and wrapped themselves in the US flag. "We're just super, super happy," Carli said.

The USWNT celebrates their World Cup win.

Carli was an energetic child.

TEAM PLAYER

Carli Anne Lloyd was born on July 16, 1982. She grew up with her brother, Stephen, and sister, Ashley, in Delran, New Jersey. Carli had a lot of energy. She didn't like to sit inside and play with toys. Her parents, Pam and Stephen, signed her up for **ballet** class. But Carli didn't like to dance either.

In high school, Carli became an impressive soccer player.

When she was five years old, Carli began playing soccer. Right away, she fell in love with the sport. She enjoyed other **team sports** too, such as basketball and baseball. But soccer was her favorite. "Everywhere I went I brought a soccer ball with me," she said. When she wasn't playing a game, she would kick the ball around with friends or by herself.

Carli played soccer at Delran High School. On the field, she stood out. Her talent for scoring goals impressed the Delran coaches. Off the field, Carli liked to have fun. She enjoyed making her friends laugh. During long runs at school, she would hide in the bushes and take shortcuts. "It was all good fun," said Carol Wolf, a friend of Carli's.

Carli began dating Brian Hollins in high school. Brian was a tall, friendly golfer. When Carli was a senior, she traveled with Brian to his family's lake cabin. Brian and his family liked to hit golf balls across the lake. It was a long shot, about 350 yards. Carli wasn't a golfer, but she decided she could make the shot. With hands wet from swimming, Carli swung with all her might. The golf club flew out of her grip and into the lake. The club was gone for good. Brian wasn't surprised by Carli's confidence. "She always thinks she can do it," he said.

Carli and Brian are planning to get married after the Olympic Games in Brazil in 2016.

In 2001, Carli graduated from Delran High School. She decided she would attend Rutgers University in New Brunswick, New Jersey. She also began playing with the Under-21 (U-21) USWNT around this time.

Carli (*center*) and two of her teammates were captains of their high school team.

Carli was one of the best athletes at Delran High School.

FASTER, STRONGER, BETTER

Carli had been the top player on her team in high school. "I was always the star," she said. At Rutgers, she proved to be one of the best players on that team too. But the U-21 USWNT was a different story. The team's **roster** included the best young players in the United States. Carli's natural talents had always allowed her to succeed without working hard. But talent alone wasn't enough for the U-21 USWNT.

Carli stretches during a training session.

In 2003, Carli had a meeting with U-21 USWNT coach Chris Petrucelli. He **cut** her from the team. She was upset. "I left the meeting crying," Carli said. She decided that she would keep playing college soccer. But she planned to quit the sport after graduating from Rutgers. "I was over it," she said.

Carli's father thought his daughter still loved soccer. She just needed someone to help her focus on fitness and becoming a better player. Her father talked to a soccer coach he knew named James Galanis. He agreed to meet with Carli.

At first, training with Galanis didn't go well. Carli showed off incredible skills with the ball. But she was out of shape. She tired quickly and didn't want to work. Galanis told her to run for 15 minutes. "I was like, uh, 15 minutes straight?" Carli said.

Galanis's training has helped Carli (*second from left*) focus throughout her career.

Slowly, Galanis helped Carli change her attitude. She realized that to be the best, she had to work harder than everyone. She put her mind to it, and soon Carli was running for 90 minutes at a time. She trained on holidays when other people relaxed. She got the most out of each exercise

Galanis helped turn Carli into one of the hardest-working players on the USWNT.

Carli attended Rutgers University in New Brunswick, New Jersey, the city shown here.

Carli earned a **degree** from Rutgers in exercise science and sports studies.

and **drill**. "I'm never going to cut it short," she said.

In 2004, Carli played her final season at Rutgers. She finished the year with 10 goals. That gave her 50 goals for her college career, the most in Rutgers history.

Carli plays in a match against China in the Algarve Cup.

OLYMPIC HERO

Carli's new approach to soccer helped her earn a place on the USWNT roster. But in her first 23 games with the team, she scored just one goal. In March 2007, the US team traveled to Portugal to play in the Algarve Cup. Carli felt strong and relaxed. She scored one goal in each of the four games. The USWNT took first place in the **tournament**. Carli was named Most Valuable Player (MVP).

Next up was the 2007 World Cup. Carli was excited to play in the most important games of her life. Soccer fans thought the USWNT could win the tournament.

Carli shows off her Algarve Cup MVP trophy and other awards.

But the United States lost to Brazil in the **semifinal** match, 4–0.

In 2008, the USWNT traveled to Beijing, China, for the Olympic Games. They beat Japan, 4–2, to reach the final match. But to win the gold medal, the United States would have to beat Brazil. The United States still felt the sting

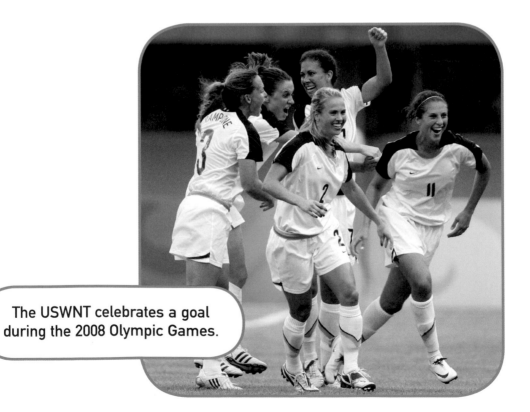

The USWNT celebrates a goal during the 2008 Olympic Games.

The USWNT poses at the Olympic Games in Beijing before their gold medal match against Brazil.

of losing to Brazil by four goals in the 2007 World Cup. Many people didn't think the USWNT stood a chance. "I hear the people talking," Carli said. "They don't think we can do it. But [the talk] just fires me up."

An ice cream shop near Carli's home created a special flavor in her honor. It's called Carli's Cake Batter Cookie Dough Kick.

Carli (*right*) takes the ball away from Brazilian player Marta.

The game against Brazil was close. The stakes were high, and neither team wanted to make a mistake. Brazilian superstar Marta fired shot after shot at the US net. Goalkeeper Hope Solo stopped every one. But on the other end of the field, Carli and her teammates couldn't score either.

The match went to **extra time**. About six

minutes into the period, Carli poked the ball to teammate Amy Rodriguez. Rodriguez fought off a Brazilian player and passed the ball right back to Carli. She pushed the ball forward and let loose with a powerful kick. The ball bounced once and landed in the corner of the net. The USWNT held on to the lead as time ran out in the game. They had won the gold medal!

Carli (*top row, right*) and some of her USWNT teammates hold up their Olympic gold medals.

Carli celebrates her first World Cup goal.

"EPIC JOURNEY"

In 2011, it was time for another crack at the World Cup. Against Colombia in their second game, Carli took control of the ball. She fired a long shot that danced through the air. The ball skipped off the fingertips of the Colombian goalkeeper and into the net. It was Carli's first World Cup goal!

The USWNT made it to the championship match against Japan. The game went to extra time with the score tied, 1–1. It was 2–2 after the extra period. That meant the World Cup would be decided by a **shoot-out**. Japan came out on top, 3–1. "Deep down inside, I thought it was our destiny to win it," Carli said. "But maybe it was Japan's."

Carli (*in white*) fires a shot at the Japanese defense in the World Cup championship.

Carli and her teammates quickly put the loss to Japan behind them. They had their sights set on the 2012 Olympics in London, England. Once again, the USWNT cruised to the gold medal game. This time, they faced Japan, the team that had just beaten them in the World Cup.

The city of Delran is proud of Carli. "When she got the winning goal in the [2012 Olympics], we had a parade for her and gave her a key to the town," said Delran's mayor.

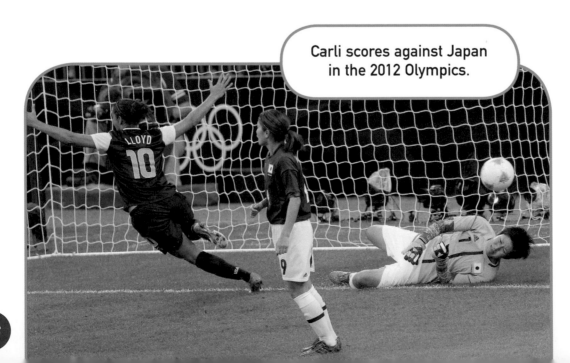

Carli scores against Japan in the 2012 Olympics.

Eight minutes into the game, US star Alex Morgan had the ball near Japan's **end line**. She lofted a pass to the front of the net. Carli leaned for a **header**. Goal! Then, in the second half, Carli took a pass near the center of the field. She raced past Japanese players and headed for the net. Carli blasted a shot for her second goal. The United States won the game, 2–1. For the second time, Carli had scored the gold medal–winning goal for her team!

Carli (*center*) and her teammates celebrate her goal against Japan at the London Olympics.

Carli shows her two Olympic gold medals.

Carli usually comes up big on the world's biggest soccer stages. But even after playing the hero in two Olympic Games, her three goals in the 2015 World Cup title match still shocked fans. The goals may have even surprised Carli herself. "I think that a lot of us needed to pinch ourselves to see if this was really happening," she said. "It was just an epic journey one will never forget."

Selected Career Highlights

2015 Helped the USWNT win the World Cup
Played her 200th international game with the USWNT
Began playing with the Houston Dash of the National Women's Soccer League

2014 Led the USWNT in goals (15) and assists (8) for the year
Scored her 50th goal with the USWNT

2012 Helped the USWNT win a gold medal at the Olympic Games
Finished third for the year in goals (15) on the USWNT

2011 Scored her first World Cup goal

2008 Helped the USWNT win a gold medal at the Olympic Games
Named US Soccer Female Athlete of the Year
Started 35 games for the USWNT, setting a new record

2007 Scored four goals in the Algarve Cup
Named Algarve Cup MVP

2006 Scored her first goal with the USWNT in an international game

2005 Made her first appearance in a game for the USWNT

2004 Played her final game with Rutgers
Finished at Rutgers as the all-time leading goal scorer (50)

2003 Was cut from the U-21 USWNT

2001 Began school at Rutgers

Glossary

ballet: a type of dance that uses light, graceful movements

cut: to remove someone from a team's roster

degree: a certificate awarded after completing a course of study at a school

drill: an exercise intended to improve skills in a specific sport

end line: the white line at both ends of a soccer field

extra time: time added to the end of a soccer match if the score is tied

goalkeeper: a player who defends the goal

hat trick: three goals scored in the same game by one person

header: a move in which a soccer player hits a ball with his or her head

roster: a list of players on a team

semifinal: the next-to-last game in a tournament

shoot-out: a competition in which teams take turns shooting the ball at the goal

team sports: sports played with teammates

tournament: a set of games held to decide the best team

Further Reading & Websites

Eason, Sarah, and Paul Mason. *Street Soccer*. Minneapolis: Lerner Publications, 2012.

Fishman, Jon M. *Abby Wambach*. Minneapolis: Lerner Publications, 2014.

Fishman, Jon M. *Alex Morgan*. Minneapolis: Lerner Publications, 2016.

Carli Lloyd's Official Website
http://www.carlilloyd.com
This website has photos and videos about Carli, information about soccer camps, and much more.

Sports Illustrated Kids
http://www.sikids.com
The *Sports Illustrated Kids* website covers all sports, including soccer.

US Women's National Team
http://www.ussoccer.com/womens-national-team
The official website of the USWNT is chock-full of content about the World Cup champions.

LERNER

SOURCE™

Expand learning beyond the printed book. Download free, complementary educational resources for this book from our website, www.lerneresource.com.

Index

Photo Acknowledgments

The images in this book are used with the permission of: © Mike Hewitt/FIFA via Getty Images, p. 4; © FRANCK FIFE/AFP/Getty Images, p. 5; © NICHOLAS KAMM/AFP/Getty Images, p. 6; © Stuart Franklin/FIFA via Getty Images, p. 8; Seth Poppel Yearbook Library, pp. 9, 10, 12, 13; AP Photo/Armando Franca, p. 14; AP Photo/Julie Jacobson, p. 15; AP Photo/Mel Evans, pp. 16, 28; © Robert Quinlan/Alamy, p. 17; AP Photo/Armando Franca, p. 18; AP Photo/Steven Governo, p. 19; © Noriko Hayakusa/Getty Images, p. 20; © MICHAEL KAPPELER/AFP/Getty Images, p. 21; © HOANG DINH NAM/AFP/Getty Images, p. 22; © Ryan Pierse/Getty Images, p. 23; AP Photo/Marcio Jose Sanchez, p. 24; AP Photo/Martin Meissner, p. 25; AP Photo/Andrew Medichini, p. 26; AP Photo/Ben Curtis, p. 27; © Lars Baron/FIFA via Getty Images, p. 29.

Front cover: © Kevin C. Cox/Getty Images.

Main body text set in Caecilia LT Std 55 Roman 16/28.
Typeface provided by Adobe Systems.